Step by Step

The Story of an Oak Tree

It Starts with an Acorn

Emma Carlson-Berne

Lerner Publications ◆ Minneapolis

Lerner Publications Company
An imprint of Lerner Publishing Group, Inc.
241 First Avenue North
Minneapolis, MN 55401 USA

For reading levels and more information, look up this title at www.lernerbooks.com.

Image credits: Westend61/Getty Images, p. 3; John Konrad/Shutterstock .com, pp. 4-5, 23; Divebatman/Shutterstock.com, p. 7; AmberFOXphoto/ Shutterstock.com, pp. 8-9; ON-Photography Germany/Shutterstock.com, pp. 10-11, 23; Svetography997/Shutterstock.com, pp. 12-13, 23; Alina Boldina/ Shutterstock.com, p. 15, 23; Akintevs/Shutterstock.com, p. 17; Photodigitaal .nl/Shutterstock.com, pp. 18-19; Bachkova Natalia/Shutterstock.com, p. 21; Julija Kumpinovica/Shutterstock.com, p. 22. Cover images: Triff/Shutterstock .com; Balinda/Shutterstock.com.

Main body text set in Mikado a Medium. Typeface provided by HVD Fonts.

Library of Congress Cataloging-in-Publication Data

Names: Carlson-Berne, Emma, 1979– author.
Title: The story of an oak tree : it starts with an acorn / Emma Carlson-Berne.
Description: Minneapolis : Lerner Publications, 2022 | Series: Step by step | Includes bibliographical references and index. | Audience: Ages 4–8 | Audience: Grades K–1 | Summary: "How does an acorn become a mighty oak tree? Readers discover the sequence of an oak tree's life cycle with step-by-step photos and clear text"– Provided by publisher.
Identifiers: LCCN 2021000223 (print) | LCCN 2021000224 (ebook) | ISBN 9781728428260 (library binding) | ISBN 9781728431666 (paperback) | ISBN 9781728430904 (ebook)
Subjects: LCSH: Oak—Life cycles—Juvenile literature. | Acorns—Juvenile literature.
Classification: LCC QK495.F14 C37 2022 (print) | LCC QK495.F14 (ebook) | DDC 583/.65—dc23

LC record available at https://lccn.loc.gov/2021000223
LC ebook record available at https://lccn.loc.gov/2021000224

Manufactured in the United States of America
1-49363-49467-4/9/2021

Oak trees stand tall.
How do they grow?

3

First, acorns drop
from an oak tree.

Then animals help to scatter the acorns.

An acorn sends
a root down into
the soil.

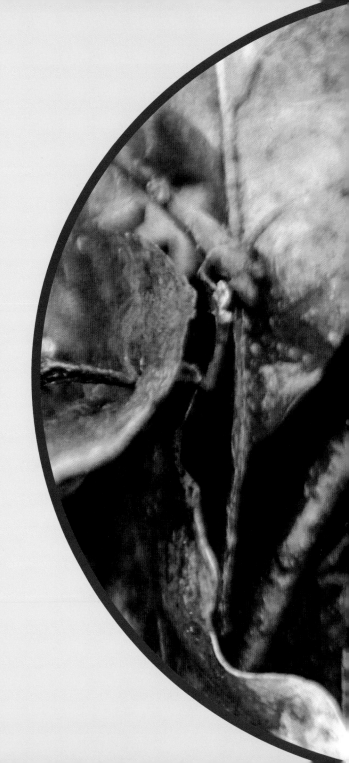

Leaves grow from
the acorn's shoot.

Next, the seedling grows bark.

The seedling grows
into a sapling.

The sapling gets
stronger and stronger.

The sapling becomes
a mature tree.

The mature tree gives shelter to animals.

New trees are born!

Picture Glossary

acorn

bark

sapling

seedling

Learn More

Neuenfeldt, Elizabeth. *Acorn to Oak Tree*. Minneapolis: Bellwether, 2021.

Taus-Bolstad, Stacy. *The Story of an Apple: It Starts with a Seed*. Minneapolis: Lerner Publications, 2021.

Tonkin, Rachel. *Acorn to Oak Tree*. New York: Crabtree, 2020.

Index